Original title:
Into the Breeze of Paradise

Copyright © 2025 Creative Arts Management OÜ
All rights reserved.

Author: Vivienne Beaumont
ISBN HARDBACK: 978-1-80581-626-3
ISBN PAPERBACK: 978-1-80581-153-4
ISBN EBOOK: 978-1-80581-626-3

The Pulse of Nature's Infinite Dance

In the forest, trees sway tight,
While squirrels practice their flight.
A bird drops a snack from above,
As if it's trying to show some love.

The flowers giggle, colors clash,
While bees zip by in a crazy dash.
The sun grins down, wearing shades so cool,
Nature's party is the silliest school.

Gliding Through Lush Miles of Calm

A rabbit nods, wearing a hat,
Sipping tea, what's up with that?
The brook is laughing, splashing about,
Who knew water had so much clout?

The butterflies waltz, what a sight,
Some get dizzy, oh what a plight!
A picnic of giggles on a sunny day,
As ants invade in a comical way.

Ethereal Adventure Awaiting

Clouds are marshmallows, soft and bright,
While rainbows dance, a colorful flight.
Fairies trip over their own tiny shoes,
As they sprinkle laughter, a delightful muse.

Mountains chuckle, watching us climb,
Chasing our dreams, oh how sublime!
With each step, we trip on our lace,
But in our hearts, we're winning the race.

The Garden of Joy in Front of Us

In the garden, veggies wear a crown,
Tomatoes blushing, no need to frown.
Carrots, in rows, gossip with peas,
Sharing secrets on the warm breeze.

Pumpkins grin, a round little lot,
While cucumbers twist, giving it a shot.
With laughter echoing, we plant our cheer,
In this funny garden, joy is near.

Dances of the Gentle Wind

The leaves are twirling in a spree,
Like dancers at a garden tea,
With each gust, they spin and glide,
A waltz that takes them far and wide.

The trees are chuckling, what a sight,
As branches shake with pure delight,
Squirrels join with acorn hats,
Bopping round like silly cats.

Echoes of a Celestial Escape

Clouds are whispering jokes up high,
While birds are laughing as they fly,
A feathered stand-up, what a blast,
Their punchlines swoop and shadows cast.

Sunshine giggles with a grin,
Tickling flowers to join in,
Hustling bees buzz with a cheer,
It's a comedy show, oh dear!

Byways of Heavenly Gales

A breeze blew in with a feather tale,
It claimed to chase the fish and whale,
With hiccups of wind, it swirled about,
Whispering secrets that made us shout.

The raindrops fell like playful sprites,
Having raves on Friday nights,
Each puddle jumped like a pogo stick,
Making giggles, quick and slick.

Lullabies of a Shimmering Dawn

Morning creaks with a sleepy yawn,
As roosters crow their funny dawn,
Snoozing cats stretch with delight,
And dream of catching mice all night.

The sun peeks in with a ray of gold,
Tickling flowers, oh so bold,
Butterflies flutter with comic grace,
A morning show, in this happy place.

Soaring Toward the Azure Horizon

A bird flew high with a goofy grin,
Spitting seeds that made me spin.
I laughed so hard, my drink went wide,
It splashed my friend who laughed and cried.

We chased clouds, wearing socks and hats,
Tripping over our friendly cats.
Each step we took was filled with cheer,
We smiled at the skies, not a single fear.

Waves of Joy in the Open Skies

Balloons floated up, a bright parade,
One popped loudly, oh, what a shade!
I painted my face, like a clown in jest,
Danced like no one was home, at my best.

With ice cream dripping down my chin,
I grinned at the sun, ready to win.
A seagull swooped down with ambitious flair,
Swiped my snack, you'd think it was fair!

Sighs from a Flourishing Haven

In a garden full of flowers bright,
I sneezed so loud, what a fright!
Bees buzzed around in a confused spin,
I waved my hands, 'Not me, my friend!'

A rabbit hopped by, wearing a tie,
Looked up at me with a curious eye.
I offered it carrots, it offered a stare,
Who knew that my lunch would become its share?

Embracing the Warmth of New Beginnings

Chasing the sun with my silly shoes,
Tripped on a rock, got tangled in blues.
I wobbled like jelly, fell on the grass,
Heard laughter around, oh what a class!

A picnic spread out, all goodies galore,
But my sandwich flew, oh, what a score!
Seagulls in flight, they considered it lunch,
But all I could do was sit and munch.

Reflections in the Cool Evening Air

As the sun dips low and blinks a wink,
I chase my shadow, what do you think?
My lemonade's gone, the ice has melted,
Was it the drink, or I'm just too swelted?

Fireflies waltz like they own the night,
I trip over laughter, oh what a sight!
The crickets giggle, chirping tunes so spry,
I lean back and wonder, why was I shy?

Shimmering Hopes in the Daylight Zephyr

A kite flies high, oh look at that go!
But still I'm grounded, my pride's in tow.
The wind laughs aloud, my hat takes the lead,
Chasing after dreams, oh yes, indeed!

Sunshine paints the grass with golden glee,
While squirrels plot mischief, just wait and see!
A picnic awaits with ants on parade,
Their tiny ambitions, I hope they don't fade.

Harmony Lost and Found in the Air

Birds sing off-key, a comedic tune,
I clap like a seal, it's a funny cartoon.
The leaves join in, rustling without fear,
As I dance with a twig, the neighbors all cheer!

Upside down thoughts, like a froggy on a spree,
Croaking out laughter, come join in, whee!
Each note a giggle, a jig in the sky,
In this breezy folly, I'm ready to fly!

Petals Adrift on a Dreamy Stream

Petals float by, in colors so bright,
I wave at a duck, who gives me a fright!
A boat made of dreams; oh what a delight,
Until I remember, my sense of sight.

The current takes charge, and I lose my hat,
As a turtle nods, thinking I'm quite fat.
We giggle in silence, this whimsical dance,
Sailing on humor, we leave it to chance!

Chasing the Light of Utopia

I chased a ray all through the day,
But my shoelaces tied in such a way.
Running fast, I took a tumble,
Landed in a flower that made me grumble.

The sunbeam giggled, said, "Oh, dear!"
"You really should watch where you steer!"
I shrugged it off, still in the hunt,
For sunshine's warmth and a cool, fun stunt.

The Garden Beneath the Skylight

In my garden, weeds wear hats,
While tomatoes whisper gossip like chitchats.
I tried to help, pulled one with glee,
It launched like a rocket, oh dear me!

The sunflowers danced, very spry,
As butterflies chuckled, soaring high.
The veggies sighed, just let them be,
While I toppled over, lost my tea.

With Each Breath of Heavenly Air

I filled my lungs with fragrant air,
While a bee buzzed by my hair!
I waved my hands, did a little spin,
But tripped on a root; where to begin?

The clouds all laughed, a cotton group,
As I rolled over like a goofing troop.
I got back up, still filled with cheer,
And bit into a pear, oh dear, oh dear!

Reverie in the Lush Expanse

In fields so wide, I dreamed of fame,
A cow came near, mooed my name!
I strut and prance, like a fancy star,
Yet stumbled on daisies, couldn't go far.

A mischievous breeze played tricks on me,
Whispering secrets from the tall oak tree.
I laughed and danced, forgetting my plight,
And shook a fist at the moon, so bright.

A Flight Through the Orchard of Wishes

In a land where wishes sprout,
Fruitful dreams are all about.
I chased a peach, it rolled away,
I laughed so hard, I lost my way.

An apple waved me over there,
Said, "Come join, it's quite the fair!"
A cherry giggled, plump and round,
As we tumbled onto the ground.

A pear dressed up in fancy shoes,
Claimed the spotlight, sang some blues.
With laughter loud, the orchard spun,
Who knew fruit could be so much fun?

So if you wander through this grove,
Just watch your step or you might strove,
For wishes here are full of glee,
And fruit just loves to dance, you see!

Hues of Joy in Whispering Winds

The wind came dressed in colors bright,
It tickled noses, oh what a sight!
With every puff, it blew a tune,
The flowers laughed from noon to moon.

A daisy whispered, "Come and play!"
While tulips twirled in grand ballet.
A breeze that painted skies with cheer,
Inviting all to gather near.

I asked a sunflower to take flight,
It opened wide, what a delight!
With petals dancing, heads held high,
It waved goodbye as it floated by.

In hues so bright, my heart would sway,
Where laughter bloomed in wild array.
Each gust a giggle, soft and sweet,
In whispered winds, life's purest treat!

Secrets Carried by the Gentle Sigh

A gentle sigh blew through the trees,
With secrets carried on the breeze.
It laughed and winked, a playful tease,
As squirrels danced, oh how they freeze!

The wind told tales of jammy pies,
And silly cats with startling eyes.
It sang of days where clouds just glide,
And chased away that pesky tide.

Underneath the giggling skies,
I found a hat that claimed to fly.
With feathers bright, it soared on high,
While I beneath just wondered why.

So listen closely, heed the sigh,
For laughter's secrets drift up high.
With every gust, there's joy to find,
A playful dance, a curious mind.

Dancing Leaves Through Open Fields

In fields where leaves all twirl and spin,
They laugh and caper, thick and thin.
The grass joins in, a green delight,
With roots that giggle, oh what a sight!

A dandelion wore a crown,
Claimed it ruled the royal town.
With clover friends, they spun around,
Creating chaos on the ground.

A tumbleweed rolled by in jest,
Proclaiming, "I'm the very best!"
It danced with glee, a lonesome sprite,
In fields of gold, it took to flight.

So when you see the leaves pursue,
Join in the fun, there's room for you!
For every gust with laughter weaves,
A joyful tale with dancing leaves.

Beyond the Fields of Easy Living

In fields where sheep wear sunglasses bright,
They gossip while munching with delight.
A cow plays chess, quite the sight,
While pigs dance around, oh what a night!

The sun is a giant pancake overhead,
With syrupy beams making all cows spread.
Chickens sing tunes while they take their bread,
And rabbits tell tales of the giant they dread.

Grasshoppers flirt with the sweet honey bees,
While turkeys strut like they've got degrees.
Life here is quirky, as fun as you please,
Where even the ants throw whimsical teas.

So join in the laughter, don't be shy,
In this land of wonders, wave goodbye.
To worries and cares, like clouds we'll fly,
We'll feast, dance, and howl, just you and I.

The Pulse of Wind and Daylight Beats

The wind sings softly, a ticklish breeze,
It tickles your nose and sways through the trees.
A squirrel in boots does a jig with ease,
While owls spin tales over cups of teas.

Sunlight is butter, drip-drip on the ground,
Worms play the banjo, their music profound.
Each note a chuckle, in shadows it's found,
Where laughter erupts, and joy knows no bound.

Clouds are the marshmallows float in the sky,
While birds wear pajamas and coo as they fly.
It's a circus of nature, no need to pry,
Just sit back and chuckle as moments go by.

So take off your shoes, dance with the grass,
Breathe in the day, let the silly times pass.
Join in the fun, let your cares turn to glass,
In the pulse of this world, let laughter amass!

Floating Stories in Hushed Lands

In quiet lands where whispers flee,
The wind tells tales of a bird named Lee.
He wears a pink hat, as odd as can be,
And dances with squirrels, so wild and free.

Nearby, the sun, like a giant's grin,
Winks at the flowers, coaxing their spin.
A snail writes poetry with a feathered pen,
While turtles giggle, they do it again.

Mountains wear glasses, mountains are wise,
They shoot out jokes wrapped in clouds, oh my!
While rivers laugh softly, a soft lullaby,
Chasing the pebbles that polished the sky.

So wander these lands with a smile so bright,
Capture the stories, let their humor ignite.
For in each little moment, the laughter takes flight,
Floating on currents, a delightful delight.

Floating on Clouds of Wonder

On fluffy clouds we leap and dive,
Chasing butterflies, feeling alive.
A goat in a tutu, what a sight!
Dancing with rainbows, oh what a delight!

Lemonade rivers, they flow sweet,
Sipping with squirrels, what a treat!
A fish in a top hat, quite the laugh,
Trying to take a splashy photograph!

Juggling with apples, oh such a grace,
A pelican joins in, just keeping pace.
Flying fish sing, "Let's have some fun!"
Under the bright and shining sun!

In a land where giggles are the law,
Even the puppies have a paw-some jaw.
So here we float, carefree and bright,
In a world where whimsy takes flight!

The Allure of Tranquil Meadows

In meadows where the dandelions play,
Cows wear sunglasses, hip hip hooray!
A sheep with a swagger, struts with pride,
Sipping mint tea with the butterfly guide.

Laughter erupts from the buzzing bees,
Tickling the flowers, just like a tease.
A duck in a bow tie quacks with flair,
While daisies bloom without a care.

The wind hums a tune, oh what a jam,
As bunnies breakdance, "Look at us, fam!"
Chasing their tails, they spin around,
Creating a whirlpool of giggles abound.

Pies cooling on branches, scent in the air,
Raccoons in bandanas, what a wild pair!
In a whimsical world of sunny glee,
Nature's ballet holds the key!

Soft Embrace of Nature's Grace

In a plush green field where snoozes reign,
A sleepy sloth sings a soft refrain.
Dewy grass tickles toes that leap,
Every dandelion dreams in its sleep.

A parrot in pajamas offers coffee,
While rabbits toast marshmallows, oh so puffy!
Giggling daisies toss and sway,
They whisper secrets, come what may.

A tortoise in roller skates zooms on by,
Challenging clouds to a race in the sky.
With a giggle and wiggle, oh what a thrill,
Nature's soft embrace gives a gentle chill.

In this land of laughter, all cares depart,
Where nature's grace fills every heart.
With a wink and a nod from the golden sun,
We dance with joy, oh what fun!

Symphony of Petals in Flight

A symphony plays where petals do twirl,
As ladybugs breakdance and whirl.
With snappy suits, they strut with pride,
Tune into nature's musical ride.

Sunbeams play checkers in the park,
While the stray kitten sings "Don't you dare bark!"
Crickets in tuxedos serenade the night,
Creating a melody that feels just right.

Mice in concert with flutes made of straw,
Compose a tune that has us in awe.
A rainbow string quartet joins in too,
Laughing as they perform, oh what a view!

In this silly place where fun takes flight,
Nature conducts with pure delight.
So let us dance and sing along,
In a world where we all belong!

Whispers of Serene Winds

A squirrel wearing shades, so bold,
Dances on branches, story unfolds.
With acorns flying in the air,
He's the king of this whimsical fair.

The clouds giggle, tickled by trees,
They share secrets carried by the breeze.
With a flip and a twirl, laughter spreads,
As flowers sway, wearing their threads.

Echoes of a Sunlit Haven

A parrot sings opera, quite off-key,
His feathered friends roll eyes, can't you see?
While bees practice jazz, strumming their legs,
The sun gives a wink, it's all just eggs.

The daisies debate, who stands the tallest,
While ants in tuxedos look the smallest.
In this garden, life is a jest,
Each moment a laugh, nature's best.

Dancer in the Gentle Zephyrs

A turtle with flair, in shades and a hat,
Moves to the rhythm, oh look at that!
He spins on his shell, in a stylish retreat,
While rabbits tap dance on their tiny feet.

A breeze lifts a dandelion, it swirls and twirls,
Sending giggles through the flowers and pearls.
The sun joins the fun, casting playful beams,
As laughter erupts, dancing with dreams.

Embrace of the Celestial Currents

A frog on a lily pad, posing with grace,
Practices yoga, what a funny face!
Meanwhile, the stars chuckle above,
As the moon gives a wink, sending love.

The wind tickles flowers, they dance in a row,
While a cat in the sun starts to put on a show.
Nature's a circus, a spectacle grand,
With giggles and chuckles across the land.

The Dance of Sun and Shade

In a world where shadows play,
The squirrels dance and cats sway.
Sunbeams twirl, a lazy cat,
Chasing shadows, imagine that!

Around the trees, the laughter blooms,
Tickling blooms in all the rooms.
The daisies giggle, the butterflies tease,
While Bernard the bee does his buzzing with ease.

A lizard slips on its little feet,
While birds sing songs that can't be beat.
The grass tickles toes with its green embrace,
As squirrels debate their nutty race.

Through the garden, giggles roam,
Nature's party feels like home.
With each step, we chance a show,
In the dance of sun and shade, we glow!

Emblem of Forgotten Joys.

A dog in shades, chasing its tail,
Thoughts of last week's pizza fail.
The cat observes with a knowing eye,
Thinking, 'Why run when you can lie?'

A breeze whispers through sails so bright,
Telling tales of a cat's great flight.
Forgotten joys in laughter's delight,
A tune for the dancing stars tonight.

Kites in the sky, all tangled up,
The kids in a frenzy, "Fill my cup!"
With soda swirls and laughter loud,
An emblem of joy, we laugh and crowd.

Capture the whimsy, the playful flair,
In the moments we cherish and share.
With silliness wrapped in a joyful bow,
Emblems of joy that continue to grow!

Whispers of the Sunlit Zephyr

A breeze tickles leaves with a laugh,
"Careful, don't make me take a photograph!"
Clouds roll by in a scruffy train,
As sunbeams wink through the rain.

A squirrel makes faces at the tree,
While the flowers spill secrets of glee.
The wind sways grass like a merry band,
With whispers that dance across the land.

Laughter rides the winds so light,
Chasing shadows, ready to fight.
The world's a stage in this sunny spree,
Together we weave a funny tapestry.

In a patch of green, the fun is vast,
Puppies chase tails, their shadows cast.
Surrounded by joy, we sing with ease,
In whispers of breezes, our worries freeze!

Dreams on the Wings of Serenity

In dreams, we're birds that fly so high,
Painting rainbows across the sky.
With silly hats and flippers too,
Swim through clouds, as dolphins do!

The moon joins in with a wink and grin,
"Did someone say we could begin?"
Stars giggle softly, a twinkle tinge,
Matching the laughter that we can binge.

Dreamboats floating down the stream,
With jellybeans and whipped cream.
We paddle through fields of cotton candy,
As the world spins round; isn't it dandy?

Through gentle dreams, where laughter sways,
Time takes a break, and smiles ablaze.
On wings of joy, forever free,
In this sweet haven, just you and me!

Seraphic Currents of Light

In a land where laughter flies,
Bananas dance beneath blue skies.
Squirrels wear the brightest bows,
Tickling leaves with their silly shows.

Cacti sing with prickly flair,
Chasing butterflies without a care.
Glowing fruits, a comical sight,
Rolling downhill in a fruit-filled flight.

Clouds wear hats from a carnival,
Tickling the ground, oh, what a brawl!
Jellybeans raining from above,
In this place, all laugh and love.

With a wink, the sun takes a bow,
Making us giggle, oh my, wow!
Together we'll twirl in pure delight,
In these currents, we take our flight.

The Sweet Passage of Freedom

A pickle boat sails on a jam sea,
With jellyfish dancing, so fancy-free.
Pickles are kings, ruling the brine,
On this voyage, it's all quite divine.

Lemonade waves splash about,
As the penguins sing and shout.
Cucumbers wear shades in the sun,
Join the fun, we're never done!

Marshmallows bounce on fluffy clouds,
Playing hopscotch, gathering crowds.
With candy flutes and chocolate beats,
We wander where glee and silliness meet.

As we sail from snack to snack,
Giggles guiding us on the track.
The taste of freedom, oh what a spree,
In this realm, we dance with glee!

Melodies of a Charmed Venture

A frog in a tux, oh what a sight,
Hopping to jazz in the pale moonlight.
Crickets strum on their tiny guitars,
While lightning bugs play with the stars.

Balloons float high, with giggles galore,
Monkeys prancing, knocking on doors.
Each step is a bop, a delightful prance,
In this world, we all take a chance.

Silly hats perched on every head,
Bouncing on clouds, no need for bed.
Lollipops twirl in the breeze so sweet,
Every note a chuckle, every beat a treat.

As melodies weave through the night,
We dance with shadows, pure delight.
In a symphony of laughter and cheer,
This charmed venture brings us near!

Elysian Breezes and Twilight Glow

Fireflies waltz in twinkling shows,
While popcorn clouds give off sweet prose.
Kites flying high with laughter to share,
Each gust a giggle, floating through air.

A cat in shades sips iced tea,
Declaring the world, its grand decree.
With marshmallow paths that melt in the sun,
In this twilight glow, we all have fun.

Bubbles floating, bursting with glee,
Painting the sky like a vibrant spree.
Giggling gnomes joining the parade,
In this bliss, our worries just fade.

With each tickle of the sunset's hand,
We wander where joy can expand.
Elysium wrapped in a silly show,
In these soft breezes, we lose our woe.

Liberation in Stillness and Light

In fields where daisies play and sway,
A cat in shades, thinks it's a buffet.
The sun does wink, a friendly tease,
While ants parade like tiny marines.

A breeze tickles, like old friend's joke,
Butterflies spin in a whimsical cloak.
Life's absurdity dances so bright,
In moments of silence, we find our light.

The Gentle Tides of Abundant Heart

A squirrel prances with a nut so grand,
While seagulls barter for a tasty rind.
The ocean's laughter, a splashy jest,
Invites all creatures to join the fest.

Waves giggle softly on sandy shore,
Tickling toes like it's hard to ignore.
Every sandcastle, a dream misplaced,
Where seagulls mock and the tides embrace.

A Voyage Through the Gentle Whirl

In the whirl of leaves, a dance-off begins,
As squirrels judge who gets the most wins.
The breeze plays DJ, spinning it fast,
While frogs croak a tune, making it last.

A leaf in the sky, a paper airplane,
Dares to dive low—oh, what a gain!
Laughter erupts as the day flies by,
In joyful chaos beneath the blue sky.

Fields of Gold and Airy Dreams

In golden fields where the daisies snore,
A chicken struts with a dream of more.
The sun winks down, 'What's your next scheme?'
While bunnies hop into a fantasy dream.

Clouds shape-shift, lending faces to see,
A pineapple wearing a cap? Quite the spree!
As laughter erupts from a patch of thyme,
Every moment here feels just sublime.

Skylarks Above a Dreamscape

Skylarks chirp, a silly tune,
Dancing high, 'neath the round moon.
A cat on a cloud, thinks it can fly,
Wonders why grasshoppers never try.

Jellybeans rain, all colors around,
The giggles of gnomes, a whimsical sound.
Marshmallow trees sway and tease,
While ants on a skateboard glide with ease.

Bubbles burst, tickle the air,
As squirrels play tag without a care.
A dreamscape's laughter, oh what a sight,
Chasing rainbows on a candy night.

Journey Beyond the Sunlit Veil

Sunlit paths where fairies trip,
On flowers' backs, they take a sip.
The sun yawns wide, lets out a grin,
While hedgehogs dance and sheep join in.

Dandelions puff in silly lines,
While squirrels debate over acorn fines.
With backpacks stuffed with glittery dreams,
They cross puddles that flow like streams.

Once upon a taco, what a delight,
Pirates serenade in the moonlight.
With laughter sprinkled on the ground,
They play hopscotch on shadows found.

Secrets Carried on the Warmth of the Day

Secrets whispered on warm summer air,
As bees do ballet without a care.
A dog on a surfboard rides the wave,
While kittens plot mischief, oh how brave!

Sunflowers gossip about the bees,
While kids chase dreams tied to the trees.
A dragon with a lollipop in tow,
Swirls and twirls, putting on a show.

Tickles from the breeze wrap around,
Laughter echoes, a joyful sound.
In this haven, silly games sprout,
With giggles and grins, there's never a doubt.

Heartbeats in the Shades of Delight

In shades where laughter softly crawls,
Daydreams bounce off painted walls.
Ice cream mountains, endless cones,
While turtles breakdance on funny phones.

With hearts that sing like bouncing balls,
They skip through the laughter, heed the calls.
Clocks made of candy, ticking so slow,
They melt in the sun, putting on a show.

As pixies spin tales of lopsided fruit,
The grass hums tunes, a playful flute.
In this whimsical realm, joy takes flight,
With heartbeats dancing in pure delight.

Chasing Shadows in the Calm

Clouds drift lazily, not a care,
While squirrels plot a silly affair.
Jumping and jiving, they chase a nut,
Life's a circus in this funny rut.

Laughter spills from a nearby brook,
As frogs don hats and start to cook.
With whispered jokes and wild ballet,
They croak the night and dance away.

Sunbeams flicker, a playful tease,
Tickling the flowers, swaying with ease.
Bees in bow ties buzz around,
Their honeyed jokes, the sweetest sound.

As shadows stretch with a yawning grin,
The day's antics are all but a win.
In this realm of giggles and cheer,
Every moment, a treasure dear.

Requiem of the Floating Blossoms

Petals drift down like ballerinas,
Twisting in air, no strict agendas.
With giggles shared on a sunlit stage,
They swirl and tumble, a floral page.

Lilies gossip in whisper tone,
While sleepy daisies snore alone.
A buttercup pulls off a prank,
Painting the roses in shades of dank.

The breeze joins in, a merry dancer,
Turning the flowers into a romancer.
In petals' chatter, there's mischief found,
Laughing as they float to the ground.

As the sun sets, the blooms conspire,
To huddle close by a leafy fire.
With each laugh, a star twinkles bright,
In this funny waltz of day and night.

The Song of Untamed Spaces

Up in the sky, the clouds are bold,
Wearing tops hats, feeling quite old.
A rogue wind steals a feathered cap,
While birds burst forth in a comical clap.

Grass blades gossip over a cup,
Sipping dew, they never shut up.
Donkeys in sunglasses, horseplay galore,
Their neighs a symphony, wanting more.

Crickets hold concerts in twilight's embrace,
With a banjo, they set a cheeky pace.
The moon winks down, a joker bright,
As the stars join in, oh what a sight!

In wild places, the humor's alive,
Where laughter and whimsy happily thrive.
Each moment a jest, a giggle, a tease,
In the untamed spaces, all hearts find ease.

Lucid Dreams on Gossamer Wings

Moths in tuxedos join the parade,
Flitting around in a dapper charade.
Butterflies giggle, jealous of style,
In this dreamland, they frolic a while.

Moonbeams play hide and seek in the night,
Casting soft shadows, a soft, silver light.
Fireflies spark, like bright little jokes,
Writing their tales with whimsical pokes.

Clouds munch stars like candy so sweet,
Squeezing out giggles from every treat.
The night hums along, a lullaby sings,
In a world where laughter takes flight on wings.

In the realm of dreams, with smiles we lay,
Floating through night, in a silly ballet.
With chuckles and sighs, we drift into bliss,
Every whisper of joy, a sparkly kiss.

Whirling Leaves and Laughter

Leaves spin around, so carefree,
Rolling with joy, just like me.
Squirrels dance in the frosty air,
Chasing their tails without a care.

The wind blew hats from my head,
My dog thought it was a bread spread!
We tumbled into a pile of cheer,
While giggles echoed, far and near.

Colors whirled in a merry swirl,
Nature giggled, oh what a whirl!
Grandpa chuckled at the merry scene,
As the neighbor yelled, "Hey, that's my bean!"

The sun dipped low, a golden view,
Caught in a dance like me and you.
In the chaos, we found delight,
In laughing leaves, from morning till night.

Where the Wildflowers Bloom

Wildflowers chuckle in sunlit fields,
Waving their petals, sharing their yields.
Bees play tag with butterflies bright,
While ants march in a silly plight.

A dandelion declares its wishes loud,
As clovers laugh, quite proud,
A lazy snail takes its time to roam,
Singing of dreams, far from home.

Bumblebees buzz with a zany tune,
Tickling the toes of a drowsy raccoon.
Laughter erupts where colors collide,
In this whimsical world, we all reside.

With jokester blooms waving hello,
Every petal's a giggle, don't you know?
Nature's comedy, a glorious scene,
In the heart of wildflower glee, we glean.

Horizon's Dappled Dreams

Clouds twirl like cotton candy fluff,
While the sun peeks, teasing enough.
Waves of laughter roll on the shore,
Where seagulls squawk, demanding more.

Sun-kissed toes in the shimmering tide,
While fish splash, wanting to hide.
A kite tangles in a curious tree,
As I giggle and shout, "Set it free!"

Shadows dance with the fading light,
As day turns to laughter, oh what a sight!
Fireflies wink with a cheeky glow,
While moonbeams skip, putting on a show.

In this dappled world where dreams collide,
Laughter leads, and worries slide.
Every moment, a snapshot of joy,
In nature's canvas, let's all enjoy!

Threads of Serenity Woven

A tapestry of whispers, soft and sweet,
Where laughter and nature joyfully meet.
Sunbeams dance in a playful thread,
Tickling the daisies, making them spread.

Waves of giggles ripple through trees,
While squirrels play tricks, just like thieves.
The brook chuckles over smooth stones,
As frogs croak jokes in silly tones.

Colors entwined, a radiant blend,
Where every moment, happiness sends.
A picnic thwarted by a cheeky crow,
Who steals my sandwich, oh no, no, no!

Yet in this scene of laughter sewn tight,
Every mishap turns into delight.
For in the threads of nature's spree,
We find a world of glee, carefree.

Visions in the Twilight Breeze

As I danced with the wind, quite a sight,
A squirrel joined in, what a hilarious flight!
With acorns for shoes, he twirled with glee,
While I tripped on my own two-left feet, oh me!

Fireflies giggled, lighting up the night,
Guiding lost dreams in their flickering flight.
A dog howled a tune, off-key yet sincere,
Making the frogs croak loud, right in my ear.

The moon winked at us from its silvery throne,
As I tried to impress with a silly tone.
But the stars just snickered, high up in the dark,
While I juggled my snacks – oh, what a lark!

So we danced through the twilight, so carefree and bold,
In a joyful mix-up, bizarre yet gold.
For in these odd moments, laughter's the key,
In twilight's embrace, wild and silly, we're free.

Serendipity in the Garden of Dreams

In a garden of flowers, I strolled with flair,
Accidentally tripped on a rather fat pear!
It rolled down the path with a comical squeak,
While daisies giggled, oh, what a peak!

A butterfly landed on my froggy hat,
I scoffed and it flapped off, all scared of my prat!
The roses turned red, not from blush but delight,
As I skipped 'round the tulips, not caring for fright.

A gnome on a mushroom gave me a wink,
He seemed quite amused at my dizzying drink.
With shadows as partners, we spun with glee,
Laughter echoing loud in this garden of me.

The sun set in colors, like paint gone awry,
While I chased my lost thoughts as they danced in the sky.

In dreams wrapped in silliness, I surely would bask,
For in this wild garden, adventure's my task.

Tides of Peace in the Open Field

In fields wide and open, I rolled like a ball,
Each tumble a giggle that echoed the call.
A cow watched in wonder, chewing with style,
As I practiced my cartwheels, though they missed by a mile.

Butterflies swooped down, curious of me,
As I tried to keep balance on an old, wobbly tree.
A breeze teased my hair, giving it flair,
While I waved to three rabbits, surprised by my dare.

They chuckled and hopped, in a synchronized way,
Jumping with laughter, what a comical sway!
The daisies applauded, swaying side to side,
In this field full of joy, where silliness won't hide.

So here in this vastness, I dance and I play,
With each silly motion, the worries drift away.
In the tides of laughter, a peace I will find,
And a wild freedom that sparks the mind.

Radiant Whispers Under Golden Skies

Beneath golden skies, my hat flies away,
As I sprint after it, trying hard not to sway.
A bird chirps a tune, it must be a joke,
While I chase my own shadow, a skipping rope.

The sun beams down, tickling my nose,
As I stumble and roll over clumps of prose.
With giggles from daisies and clouds that just grin,
I dance in the sunlight, oh, where do I begin?

A lizard gives advice, "Just enjoy the scene,"
While I stumble and fumble like a clumsy machine.
The breeze whispers secrets, a tickle and tease,
As I follow the laughter and jump with ease.

So here in the warmth, in these radiant hues,
I laugh at my foibles, with nothing to lose.
Underneath laughter's sky, wild and airy,
We find joy in the dance, oh so merry!

Serenade of the Golden Fields

In fields of gold, I slipped in mud,
Chasing butterflies, 'til I went thud.
The cows all laughed, they knew my plight,
As I rolled around, a silly sight.

Sunflowers danced, looking quite grand,
I tried to join, but fell on my hand.
The bees all buzzed a comical tune,
While I shook off dirt, under the moon.

Oh, frolicsome winds, they whisked my hat,
I chased it down, now I look like a cat.
With ribbons and flowers tangled in hair,
I laugh and shout, without a care.

In golden fields, my antics unfold,
Immortalized in stories bold.
Every trip, every tumble and fall,
A serenade shared, enjoyed by all.

Voyage Through Eden's Embrace

On a raft of leaves, I sailed 'round the bend,
With my snack of apples, to share with my friend.
Then a duck ambushed, quacking with glee,
Swiped my sandwich, oh woe is me!

I waved my arms, a captain so brave,
But tripped on a turtle, oh what a save!
The fish laughed hard, giving thumbs up,
As I splashed around for my lost lunch cup.

Garden gnomes peeked, with a cheeky grin,
As I transformed the splashing into a win.
We danced with daisies, a wiggly cheer,
Riding the waves with nothing to fear.

Voyaging forth, embraced by the green,
Bumbling and laughing, we lived like a dream.
So here's to the ducks, the fish, and the sun,
In Eden's warm arms, we found all the fun.

Murmurs of the Blissful Horizon

On a hilltop high, I planted my flag,
But a gust of wind made my trousers snag.
With a split and a puff, I tumbled down,
The horizon chuckled, without a frown.

Clouds whipped by, looking quite silly,
As I rolled in the grass; oh so frilly!
The daisies whispered, "What a funny sight!"
As I danced with the butterflies till night.

A squirrel hollered, gathering his loot,
I offered him berries, and jumped on a root.
With a flick and a twist, he dashed off fast,
Leaving me giggling, a memory to last.

The horizon murmured, "Join the parade!"
So I skipped and I hopped, a grand escapade.
Mirthfully lost in my tumble and cheer,
In blissful wonders, I conquered fear.

Tides of Joyful Liberation

On sandcastles high, I proudly sat proud,
When a wave crashed in, washed my hopes loud.
A mermaid grinned, with a flick of her tail,
While I scrambled up, in a comical flail.

Beneath the sun, I found seashells bright,
But slipped on a crab; oh, what a fright!
Rolling in laughter, the seagulls took notes,
As I donned a seaweed hat, giggling with quotes.

With sand in my toes, I built one more dream,
And launched my stick boat with a triumphant scream.
The tides pulled it back, and I couldn't agree,
A life of mishaps is the best, can't you see?

Joyful liberation in waves I now find,
As I splash and I laugh, leaving worries behind.
For amidst every tumble, each slip and each slide,
Are the tides of my heart, where true joy does abide.

A Haven Found on Serene Currents

A duck in a hat could steal the show,
He waddles with swagger, a real-life pro.
The fish in their suits dance with such flair,
While crickets hold concerts for all who care.

The lilies are laughing, they shimmer and sway,
As frogs strike a pose in the warm sunny ray.
Each breeze tells a joke that rains down like spritz,
With butterflies chuckling in comical wits.

A picnic of clouds spills jellybeans bright,
Fireflies giggle, they glow in the night.
With marshmallow pillows that float in the air,
This silly paradise, you can't help but stare.

So come join the fun in this whimsical land,
Where giggles float freely, just take my hand.
Bring your gleeful spirit and let it be known,
In this joyful refuge, you never alone.

Taste of Infinity in the Soft Wind

A squirrel on a kite chases dreams in the sky,
He nibbles on nuts while his friends zoom by.
The breeze whispers secrets that no one can hold,
Like jellybean wishes that shimmer like gold.

A cat in a hammock reads tales from afar,
While worms take a stroll in the light of a star.
With laughter for breakfast, they feast on delight,
The charm of this romp keeps the world feeling bright.

Dragonflies twirl in a silly ballet,
While ants play charades in a fast-packed array.
With smiles like rainbows that color the ground,
In this place so absurd, true joy can be found.

So take a big bite of this gust of fresh air,
Where giggles and munchies are always a pair.
In a whirlwind of fun where laughter is king,
The taste of infinity makes your heart sing.

Sweet Embrace of the Open Meadows

A goat with a grin chews grass with such flair,
Each chew is a giggle, light-hearted and rare.
With daisies doing cartwheels in sunsplashed delight,
And bees breaking into their dance every night.

The sunflowers sway, gossiping under their hats,
While rabbits wear sunglasses, chilling with bats.
As laughter erupts from the ticklish tall grass,
Nature's own venue, where every joke's brass.

A pig with a dream aspires to be free,
He's planning a splash in the old oaken tree.
With the wind as his wingman, the sky's not the limit,
He'll leap with a snort and fit the whole in it.

So lay on the ground where the colors all blend,
In a meadow so merry, you'll make a new friend.
Here joy's in the air, a fragrance so sweet,
You might just get lost in this life's silly beat.

Breathe in the Calmness of Utopia

A llama in sunglasses lounges in style,
He sips on sweet tea and grins with a smile.
While clouds play hopscotch over the trees,
And giggle-filled breezes deliver the tease.

A turtle in flip-flops takes strolls on the beach,
With starfish who sing notes within perfect reach.
As kites shaped like fish dance on waves ever soft,
You can't help but laugh, let your funny side loft.

A dance of the daisies arrives with the morn,
With everyone joining, it feels like a storm.
While frogs in tuxedos preside over charms,
Each laugh is a magic that sways and disarms.

So take in the calmness wrapped in a grin,
In this whimsical land it's a riot within.
Just breathe in the laughter, let joy be your guide,
In a world full of giggles, love's never denied.

Beneath the Arch of Luminous Skies

Beneath the arch of glowing light,
The bees wear tiny hats so bright.
Frogs jump in and do the jig,
While crickets play a tune, oh dig!

The clouds all giggle, float and sway,
As raindrops dance the day away.
A sunbeam slips, it's on a slide,
And banana peels take folks for a ride!

Joyful laughter fills the air,
With twinkling eyes, the flowers stare.
A squirrel spins a tale so grand,
While daisies cheer in perfect band.

So let's all skip and twirl about,
With silly hats, there's never doubt!
In this place where fun can grow,
We'll laugh and play, now let's go!

Horizon's Tender Kiss

At dawn, the sun wakes with a yawn,
And dances 'round the sleepy lawn.
A chicken struts, it thinks it's cool,
While pigs learn ballet by the pool!

The waves wear shades, they splash and crash,
And seagulls dive with flamboyant flash.
A crab attempts a graceful spin,
While seaweed wigs are worn with grin.

Fishermen try to catch a wave,
But fish just laugh, they misbehave!
A dolphin smirks, flips in the air,
While jellyfish float in perfect flair.

Beneath this sky, we laugh and cheer,
With each small joy, we have no fear.
Let's paint our dreams in silly hues,
And dance beneath the morning views!

Unfolding in Nature's Embrace

In nature's arms, we spin and twirl,
As butterflies in tutus swirl.
A grasshopper leaps like it's in flight,
While ants wear shades, they're quite the sight!

Trees tickle each other with their leaves,
And gather gossip among the heaves.
A woolly sheep sports a bright pink tie,
While swirling with the wind, oh my!

The daisies gossip, oh what a scene,
About that one bee who's so keen.
They say he's got a date tonight,
With a flower who's just out of sight!

As clouds break into giggly fits,
We stomp in puddles, avoiding fits.
In this embrace, forever we'll play,
With nature's joy leading the way!

Canvas of Freed Fantasies

Upon a canvas, colors collide,
As polka-dotted cars take a ride.
A sleepy cat dreams of the moon,
While cupcakes sing a merry tune!

The rainbows stretch like silly strings,
As unicorns grace us with their wings.
Mermaids laugh in shades of pink,
As jellybeans dance near the brink.

With paintbrushes made of candy cane,
We splash with glee in a sugary rain.
The starfish surf on waves of cream,
As a joyous chorus splits the seam!

In our own world, let's twirl and spin,
With bouncy hearts, we dive right in.
For laughter's our brush, with colors so bright,
We'll paint our dreams, oh what delight!

Chasing Echoes of Gentle Whispers

In the park where ducks do waddle,
I tripped on a ball and gave a cackle.
The echoes of laughter fill the space,
As squirrels judge my awkward grace.

With whispers of candy in the air,
I find a refund in the fair!
Balloons float high and so does my dream,
While ice cream drips and causes a scream.

I chase after tunes that float like clouds,
While dogs run past in joyous crowds.
Each giggle and snort, a new delight,
As I tumble again, lost in sheer flight.

At dusk, we laugh, turning silly tricks,
Mixing joy like a cake that sticks.
Echoed giggles, a never-ending race,
In the park where smiles find their place.

Mornings Wrapped in Silken Dreams

The sun peeks in, a laughing sprite,
Coffee spills like morning's light.
Pajamas dance as I trip on the floor,
While my toast declares it's ready for more.

Chasing my cat, who seems so wise,
I question if she wears a disguise.
With a leap and a pounce, she steals my seat,
Now I'm the one to admit defeat!

Eggs on the stove begin to sing,
But I'm too busy zigzagging in spring.
Worms wiggle as I step outside,
I giggle like they're hiding a ride.

Wrapped up tight in whims and charms,
Determined to avoid the morning alarms.
A constant chase, a silly scene,
In the joyous light, I'm a breakfast queen!

A Sky of Hope with Every Breath

The clouds look like cotton candy spun,
As I skip along, laughing for fun.
Kites overhead, doing flips in the air,
While I trip over my own two feet, unaware.

Birds are chirping tunes of cheer,
While I dance like a goat, no fear!
My hat flies off into the blue,
Now I'm a hatless wonder, who knew?

With each breath, a whimsical dream,
Bubbles float by, glistening like cream.
I chase them down with a flourish of grace,
And bump into kids, all in the race.

In this vast expanse, my heart takes wing,
As laughter rings out, a joyful fling.
A sky full of hope, light as a feather,
With every breath, I dance and tether.

Freefalling into the Serenity of Now

I jumped off the swing, thought it was safe,
But landed like a pancake, all out of place.
Giggles erupt as friends gather round,
In this splat of a moment, pure joy found.

A frisbee flies, a comet in flight,
As I dodge and weave, what a silly sight!
My hair is a mess, my shirt's inside out,
But laughter is what I'm really about.

Collecting my thoughts like marbles in jar,
I tumble and roll like a falling star.
Every laugh is a treasure, each tear a cheer,
In the chaos of play, there's nothing to fear.

With friends by my side, we soar and we glide,
In this moment of joy, there's nothing to hide.
Freefalling into the now, let's go with the flow,
In this mad, merry world, we'll steal the show!

Sunbeam Trails in the Morning Mist

A squirrel wearing shades, quite a sight,
Dancing on branches, oh what a delight!
Chasing sunbeams, in playful grace,
Leaves whisper laughter, in this wild space.

Pancakes flip-flop in the air,
While flowers giggle without a care.
A bee takes a selfie, strikes a pose,
Nature's fun circus, who really knows?

Frogs croak their tunes, a concert at dawn,
Bouncing on lily pads, laughing till they yawn.
Butterflies flutter in polka-dot styles,
Turning the meadows into laughter miles.

As clouds drift by with a chuckle or two,
The sun spills gold, painting skies blue.
This morning mist, a canvas of cheer,
In the hilarious charms that nature holds dear.

Serene Thoughts in a Dappled World

In a field of daisies, a cow takes a nap,
Wearing a flower crown, what a funny flap!
A snail on a mission, racing the sun,
Says, 'I'll win this race, though I weigh a ton!'

Chickens in top hats strut with such flair,
While ducks in tuxedos, slide down with care.
A breeze comes to giggle, ruffling their hair,
Nature's own fashion, no need to compare.

Sunlight dapples, paints shadows with glee,
As bees mix their honey with some sweet tea.
A hedgehog in sneakers, rolling with style,
Turns every stroll into a comical mile.

In this world of quirks, peace lies in jest,
Where every odd moment becomes a fun fest.
Serenity dances, a whimsical swirl,
In the laughter that bubbles in this dappled world.

Horizon's Embrace and Timeless Whispers

The horizon beams, all pink and bright,
With sunflowers winking, what a sight!
Clouds play chess, while the sun sips tea,
    Reigning over all, in a jolly decree.

A turtle in shades takes a leisurely stroll,
While the goats cheer loudly, 'Who's got the goal?'
Whispers in laughter pass from tree to tree,
As the butterflies join in, to giggle with glee.

The waves high-five the shore with a giggle,
Seagulls crack jokes, oh how they wiggle!
Even the sand seems to chuckle and sway,
At the playful time spent at the end of the day.

As shadows stretch long, and dusk paints the land,
Every moment is magic, just like we planned.
Horizon smiles wider, with each radiant star,
In whispers of laughter, we'll wander afar.

A Canvas Painted by the Winds

The winds waltz in, with colors ablaze,
Painting the skies in whimsical ways.
A kite shaped like pizza gets caught in a tree,
While children laugh hard, 'Hey, look at me!'

Clouds turn into llamas, fluffy and fun,
They prance through the heavens, a miraculous run.
The drizzle joins in, just tickling toes,
As puddles reflect all the giggles that flow.

The trees tell a story, branches like arms,
As squirrels reenact the dance of their charms.
A painter with feathers dips in the sky,
Crafting a masterpiece, oh my, oh my!

With each gust of laughter, the world spins around,
Colors mix wildly, in joy they are found.
A canvas created by whimsy and cheer,
In the dance of the winds, we all want to stay near.

The Silence of a Soft Landing

I landed with a thud, so not quite soft,
My wings all askew, not aloft.
I'm greeted by a llama, quite absurd,
Whispering secrets, not one word heard.

The grass tickles my toes, oh what a sight,
A disco ball sun that shines so bright.
My pal the parrot, he starts to dance,
Pulls me along in a feathery trance.

Cacti wear hats, they're having a ball,
While rabbits play poker, not worried at all.
I join their game, oh what a mistake,
I owe a big chip, a fluffy cupcake!

With giggles and grins, I'll never forget,
This quirky soft landing, my best set yet!
Llama waves goodbye, with a wink of his eye,
Until next time's arrival, I bid them goodbye!

Lost in the Embrace of Celestial Skies

Up in the clouds where I fancied to play,
I stumbled on a group of clouds at bay.
They looked so fluffy, like cotton candy,
But they were quite moody, a bit too dandy.

One cloud whispered tales of a stormy plight,
While another proposed a bubblegum fight.
Their laughter echoed like a tickling breeze,
I laughed so hard, I fell to my knees.

Stars joined in with their twinkling jokes,
As meteors joked about fiery hoaxes.
"Catch me if you can!" one boldly stated,
But oh dear, I tripped and feel quite outdated.

Floating around in this mix-up of bliss,
Moonbeams and giggles, I can't help but miss.
Yet in this chaotic cosmic carnival, I fly,
Embraced by the skies, oh how time does fly!

Heartbeats in the Heart of Nature

In the woods where squirrels wear shades so neat,
Acorns bounce like soccer balls, oh what a feat.
I tried to join their game, but whoops! Oh dear,
Tripped over a mushroom, quite the veneer.

A wise old owl hooted, "What's this commotion?"
While frogs croaked laughter, causing a notion.
Bees in bow ties buzz past with flair,
Announcing my fall with such royal care.

The trees giggled softly, their leaves a-flitter,
As I danced with a hedgehog, it jumped, oh our glitter!
We spun around 'til the stars felt offbeat,
A conga line formed, what a joyful feat!

Nature chuckles in its gentle embrace,
With heartbeats of laughter keeping the pace.
In this woodland symphony, alive and free,
I found my funny home, oh can't you see?

The Serene Pathway to Tranquility

Oh, how serene is this winding lane,
Where I met a snail offering champagne.
He said, "Take a sip, it'll lighten your load,"
I laughed so hard, we both nearly exploded!

A raccoon in boots played a guitar,
Strumming tunes that travelled far.
Singing of treasures found in a bin,
While I bobbed my head and joined in the din.

Clouds drifted by in a leisurely pace,
With floating sunflowers, a magical place.
Tomatoes in tutus twirled with delight,
As fireflies played hopscotch, what a sight!

Through giggles and cheer, I strolled on my way,
On this path of laughter, I couldn't delay.
With each careful step, I found peace and glee,
In the silly serenity that welcomed me!

www.ingramcontent.com/pod-product-compliance
Lightning Source LLC
Chambersburg PA
CBHW072119070526
44585CB00016B/1501